WILD ANIMALS

COPPERHEADS

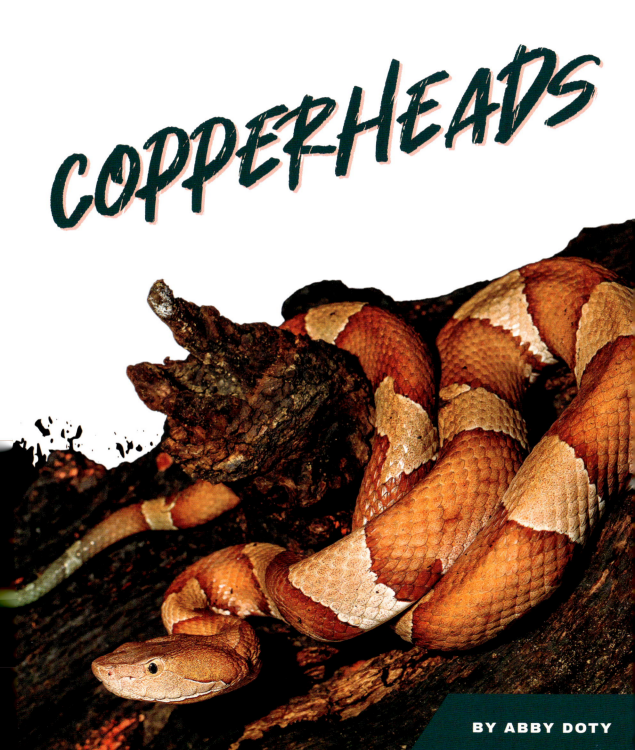

BY ABBY DOTY

WWW.APEXEDITIONS.COM

Copyright © 2026 by Apex Editions, Mendota Heights, MN 55120. All rights reserved. No part of this book may be reproduced or utilized in any form or by any means without written permission from the publisher.

Apex is distributed by North Star Editions:
sales@northstareditions.com | 888-417-0195

Produced for Apex by Red Line Editorial.

Photographs ©: Shutterstock Images, cover, 1, 4–5, 6–7, 12–13, 19, 20, 25, 26–27, 29; Joe McDonald/Science Source, 8; iStockphoto, 10–11, 14, 15, 21, 22–23; Court Harding/iNaturalist, 16–17; John Mitchell/Science Source, 18; Alan Rockefeller/iNaturalist, 24

Library of Congress Control Number: 2024952636

ISBN
979-8-89250-547-5 (hardcover)
979-8-89250-583-3 (paperback)
979-8-89250-651-9 (ebook pdf)
979-8-89250-619-9 (hosted ebook)

Printed in the United States of America
Mankato, MN
082025

NOTE TO PARENTS AND EDUCATORS

Apex books are designed to build literacy skills in striving readers. Exciting, high-interest content attracts and holds readers' attention. The text is carefully leveled to allow students to achieve success quickly. Additional features, such as bolded glossary words for difficult terms, help build comprehension.

CHAPTER 1
FINDING FOOD 4

CHAPTER 2
STRONG SNAKES 10

CHAPTER 3
HIDDEN HUNTERS 16

CHAPTER 4
LIFE CYCLE 22

COMPREHENSION QUESTIONS • 28
GLOSSARY • 30
TO LEARN MORE • 31
ABOUT THE AUTHOR • 31
INDEX • 32

CHAPTER 1

FINDING FOOD

A copperhead snake lies on the forest floor. It hears something move nearby. The snake flicks out its tongue. It smells a mouse.

A copperhead's tongue brings in air for the snake to smell.

Suddenly, the snake lunges. Its fangs sink into the mouse. **Venom** flows into the small animal.

FAST FACT

A copperhead's venom breaks down red blood cells. That can hurt or kill other animals.

A copperhead's fangs get replaced several times throughout the snake's life.

The copperhead holds the mouse's head in its mouth. Soon, the venom kills the mouse. The snake has its meal.

MASSIVE MOUTHS

A copperhead's mouth has a special bone. This bone allows the snake's mouth to open extra wide. A copperhead can also move its **organs** around. That makes room inside the snake's body.

◀ Copperheads usually swallow animals whole.

CHAPTER 2

STRONG SNAKES

Most copperheads are 2 to 3 feet (0.6 to 0.9 m) long. The snakes have thick bodies and strong **muscles**. Their heads are shaped like triangles.

The copperhead is named after the color of its head. The scales are reddish-brown, similar to copper.

A copperhead's body has light-brown scales. But there are also dark-brown markings on its back. The markings look like **hourglasses**.

FAST FACT
A copperhead's markings help the snake blend in with dead leaves.

Copperheads often hide among fallen leaves, logs, and branches.

More than 100,000 copperheads live in North America.

Copperheads live in eastern and central parts of the United States. Some live in northern Mexico, too. The snakes usually live in wooded areas.

BIG BITERS

Many copperheads live near humans. The snakes sometimes bite people. In fact, copperheads account for more bites than any other snake in the United States. The bites hurt, but they are usually not deadly to humans.

Copperheads tend to keep to themselves. But the snakes may attack if startled.

CHAPTER 3

Hidden Hunters

Throughout the spring and fall, copperheads are active during the day. In the summer, the snakes hunt at night. That helps them stay cool.

Copperheads have large meals. So, most copperheads eat just 10 to 12 times a year.

A copperhead can swallow an animal up to three times the size of its head.

Copperheads hunt alone. Usually, the snakes hide and wait. They attack when an animal comes near.

FAST FACT

Copperheads are carnivores. The snakes eat mostly mice, birds, lizards, and frogs.

Copperheads often eat insects, such as cicadas.

Copperheads may climb trees while hunting.

Sometimes, copperheads move around to hunt. The snakes use hearing, smell, and vision to track **prey**. Copperheads can also sense other animals' body heat.

PIT SENSORS

A copperhead has two pits between its nose and eyes. These pits **detect** heat and changes in temperature. That helps the snake find prey in the dark.

Several types of snakes have pit sensors. These snakes are known as pit vipers.

CHAPTER 4

LIFE CYCLE

In spring, copperheads travel to feeding areas. Many **mate** during this time. Male snakes may fight one another over females.

Sometimes, male copperheads must fight females. Females only mate with males that don't back down.

Only about 20 percent of copperhead babies live longer than a year.

The snakes return to their **dens** in fall. Females give birth to live babies. Copperheads are born with fangs. They live and hunt on their own right away.

Tricky Tails

Young copperheads have bright green or yellow tails. The tails look like caterpillars. Lizards and frogs think the tails are food. They come close. Then the young snakes attack.

A young copperhead may wiggle its tail to make it look like a living caterpillar.

Copperheads begin to have their own babies at four years old.

Copperheads **hibernate** in the winter. They rest together in groups. Often, the snakes return to the same dens each year. Then, the cycle starts again the next spring.

FAST FACT
Copperheads can live up to 18 years in the wild.

COMPREHENSION QUESTIONS

Write your answers on a separate piece of paper.

1. Write a few sentences explaining the main ideas of Chapter 2.

2. Would you like to have a copperhead snake living near your home? Why or why not?

3. What color might a young copperhead's tail be?
- **A.** green
- **B.** brown
- **C.** red

4. Why do copperheads hunt at night during the summer?
- **A.** Nighttime gets too hot during the summer.
- **B.** Daytime gets too cold during the summer.
- **C.** Daytime gets too hot during the summer.

5. What does **lunges** mean in this book?

*Suddenly, the snake **lunges**. Its fangs sink into the mouse.*

   A. slowly moves away from something
   B. quickly moves toward something
   C. stays in the same place

6. What does **carnivores** mean in this book?

*Copperheads are **carnivores**. The snakes eat mostly mice, birds, lizards, and frogs.*

   A. animals that eat other animals
   B. animals that eat only plants
   C. animals that eat every day

Answer key on page 32.

GLOSSARY

dens
The homes of wild animals.

detect
To sense or find something.

hibernate
To rest or sleep through the winter.

hourglasses
Tools with two glass sections that are used to tell time. Sand flows from an upper section to a lower section.

mate
To form a pair and come together to have babies.

muscles
Parts of the body that help with strength and movement.

organs
Parts of the body that do certain jobs.

prey
Animals that are hunted and eaten by other animals.

venom
A poison made by an animal and used to bite or sting prey.

BOOKS

Nguyen, Suzane. *Copperheads*. Bellwether Media, 2025.
Stevenson, Paul. *Deadly Snakes*. Hungry Tomato, 2024.
Terp, Gail. *Copperheads*. Black Rabbit Books, 2021.

ONLINE RESOURCES

Visit **www.apexeditions.com** to find links and resources related to this title.

ABOUT THE AUTHOR

Abby Doty is a writer, editor, and booklover from Minnesota.

INDEX

B
biting, 15

C
carnivores, 19

D
dens, 24, 27

F
fangs, 6, 24

H
hunting, 16, 18, 20, 24

M
Mexico, 14
mouth, 9
muscles, 10

O
organs, 9

P
prey, 20–21

S
scales, 12

T
tails, 25
tongue, 4

U
United States, 14–15

V
venom, 6, 9

ANSWER KEY:
1. Answers will vary; 2. Answers will vary; 3. A; 4. C; 5. B; 6. A